Why Pocket Posters?

Daydream Education, the UK's leading provider of educational posters, has developed a versatile range of colourful and engaging study guides that break down barriers to learning and encourage independent learning.

Small in size, huge in content!

Designed to engage learners, Pocket Posters simplify important KS2 content into bitesize chunks of information to improve pupils' understanding and boost confidence.

> **"**Daydream's Pocket Posters present information in a clear and concise way that is easy for pupils to understand. The books have improved pupils' confidence and enabled them to communicate their ideas effectively across all curriculum subjects. **"**
>
> **A Chapman**
> **English Teacher**

Daydream Education | Unit 1 | Central Park | Western Avenue | Bridgend | CF31 3RH
Tel: 0844 800 1660 | Fax: 0844 800 1664 | www.daydreameducation.co.uk
Chris Malcolm Ltd. t/a Daydream Education. Registered in England and Wales. Company No: 04216204

Contents

Spelling (continued)

Reading and Writing

Nouns

Nouns are words that name things such as objects, animals, places and people.

Common

Common nouns are words that refer to an object, person or place.

ball	**boy**	**library**
The ball is round.	The boy was lonely.	It is an old library.

Proper

Proper nouns are words that name a particular place, person or object.

France (place)	**Mike (person)**	**Eiffel Tower (object)**

A proper noun will always start with a capital letter.
Mike went to France to visit the Eiffel Tower.

Collective

Collective nouns are words that refer to a group or collection of people, animals, objects or places.

crowd	**troop**	**bunch**

The crowd watched as the troop of monkeys tussled over the bunch of bananas.

Abstract

Abstract nouns are words that refer to emotions, thoughts or ideas.

love	**anger**	**passion**
Jessica knew her love for Jordan was real.	He was filled with anger.	She has a passion for swimming.

Noun Phrases

A noun phrase is a group of words that acts like a noun.
It consists of a noun and other words that modify it.

The boy tripped over his sister's bag.	The birds flew over those trees.

You can create expanded noun phrases by adding more information:

The clumsy boy tripped over his little sister's new bag.	The flock of birds flew over those apple trees.

 daydream
EDUCATION

Pronouns

Pronouns are words used to avoid repeating a noun.

Common Pronouns

| I | you | he/she | it | we | they | me | him/her | us | them |

We went to the concert, but you forgot the tickets.

Possessive pronouns show ownership.

| my | your | his/her | its | our | their | mine | yours | his/hers | ours | theirs |

Mason took my bag and hid it under his desk.

See how pronouns have been used to improve the following sentences.

Christopher played on Christopher's computer until the computer broke.

Christopher played on his computer until it broke.

Emma picked up the ball and kicked the ball to Theo, Emma's friend.

Emma picked up the ball and kicked it to Theo, her friend.

The musician was annoyed because the musician had not tuned the musician's guitar.

The musician was annoyed because she had not tuned her guitar.

Using Pronouns for Effect

Pronouns are often used by writers to persuade or engage their audience.

First Person Pronouns such as we, our and us are used to include the audience. In the example, we is used to emphasise unity and a common purpose.

"We will fight them on the beaches."
- Winston Churchill

Second Person Pronouns such as you and yours address the reader personally and are often used in persuasive writing. In the example, you presumes a connection between the writer and audience.

"You must try these new Chocbits."

Third Person Pronouns such as they and them are used to distance the writer from the audience or what is being written about. In the example, they and their are used to distance the writer from the statement.

"They did not do their job properly."

Adjectives

Adjectives are words that are used to describe nouns – they tell you more about something.

Adjectives add detail and can make your descriptions more interesting. They are usually placed directly before the noun that they are describing.

Ella has an **enormous** meal for breakfast.

The **ferocious** storm caused **significant** damage.

Her **stylish new** car has **incredible** acceleration.

In some sentences the adjectives are placed after the noun:

The gate was **old** and **rusty**.

Comparative Adjectives

Adjectives that compare two nouns usually end in **er**.

Amy is **taller** than Joseph.

Harry is **quicker** than his brother.

The jeans are **cheaper** than the trainers.

When an adjective has more than two syllables, **more** or **most** are used before the adjective.

Imagination is **more important** than knowledge.

Jess thinks football is **more exciting** than cricket.

Adjectives that compare more than one noun usually end in **est**. However, if the base word ends in y, remove the y and add **iest**.

Russia is the **largest** country in the world.

Aaron has the **heaviest** bag.

Remember! Adjectives are used to describe nouns, not verbs.

daydream
EDUCATION

Verbs

Verbs are doing or being words – they tell you what someone or something is doing.

Some verbs express **physical** or **mental** actions.

Abby rides her bike to school.

Henry saved the ball from the goal.

I guessed the correct answer.

Rahim likes his new television.

Some verbs express a state-of-being.
The following table shows different forms of the verb to be.

	Past	Present	Future
I	was	am	will be
You	were	are	will be
He/She	was	is	will be
It	was	is	will be
We	were	are	will be
They	were	are	will be

I am older than my brother.

You are lost.

They were late for work.

Simon will be a singer.

State-of-being verbs are often used with main verbs:

I was playing tennis.   She is drinking all of the juice.   They will be walking home.

Modal Verbs

A modal verb comes before another verb to change its meaning.

will   shall   can   might   should   must   may   could   would

They can tell you how possible or necessary something is:

I will go to the concert.   They can fix the car.   I must remember my lunch.

Verb Tenses

The tense of a verb tells you when it happened. There are three basic verb tenses: past, present and future.

Notice how the different verbs change in each tense.

Subject	Simple Past	Simple Present	Simple Future
I	I **jogged** to college.	I **jog** to college.	I **shall** jog to college.
You	You **played** the drums.	You **play** the drums.	You **will play** the drums.
He	He **listened** to the radio.	He **listens** to the radio.	He **will listen** to the radio.
She	She **dyed** her hair.	She **dyes** her hair.	She **will dye** her hair.
It	It **worked** well.	It **works** well.	It **will work** well.
We	We **tried** to win.	We **try** to win.	We **shall** try to win.
They	They **ran** fast.	They **run** fast.	They **will run** fast.

In the present tense, most regular verbs do not change. However, when the subject is *he*, *she*, *it*, or a ***person's name***, an **s** is added to the verb.

Traditionally, **shall** is used instead of **will** with *I* and *we*.

Unless it is intentional, ensure you do not change between tenses in your sentences!

Damon **caught** the ball and then **throws** it to Ben. ✗

Damon **caught** the ball and then **threw** it to Ben. ✓

In addition to the simple past, present and future tenses, there are nine other tenses.

Past Continuous	Present Continuous	Future Continuous
We **were playing** tennis.	We **are playing** tennis.	We **will be playing** tennis.

Past Perfect	Present Perfect	Future Perfect
He **had played** tennis.	He **has played** tennis.	He **will have played** tennis.

Past Perfect Continuous	Present Perfect Continuous	Future Perfect Continuous
They **had been playing** tennis.	They **have been playing** tennis.	They **will have been playing** tennis.

Adverbs

Adverbs are describing words that tell you more about verbs.

Adverbs provide more information about verbs and can be placed at the start, middle or end of a sentence.

Cautiously, he crept into the room.

The owl slowly turns its head.

She sang the song beautifully.

Many, but not all, adverbs end in 'ly'.

Adverbs are used to describe how, when, how often and where something is happening.

How?	When?	How often?	Where?
quickly	lately	frequently	above
cruelly	recently	constantly	inside
angrily	again	daily	there
nervously	after	sometimes	away

Adverbs can be used to describe other word classes such as **adjectives** and **other adverbs**:

Alisha was very excited about her birthday party.

The weather forecast is almost always wrong.

Adverbials are words, phrases or clauses that act as adverbs.

CINEMA

I met Jessica at the cinema.

As soon as he could, he jumped off the boat.

He ran as fast as possible.

When an adverbial is placed at the beginning of a sentence, it is called a 'fronted adverbial'.

Prepositions

Prepositions are words that tell you where, or when, things happen. They are used with nouns or pronouns.

Prepositions of Time

Prepositions of time tell you **when** something is happening.

before	after	until	at	since	on	during

Isabelle's birthday party is being held in the Village Hall **on** Sunday **at** 4 p.m. **During** the party, there will be music, dancing and games.

Prepositions of Place

Prepositions of place tell you the **position or direction** of something.

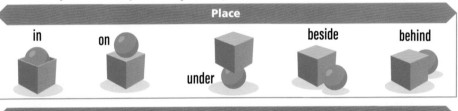

Place

in   on   under   beside   behind

Position

through   up   down   across   around

The dog ran **around** the garden whilst the cat hid **behind** the fence.

Some words can function as **prepositions of time or place**.

Centuries/Decades/Years/Months		Countries/Cities/Towns/Villages
the 1900s the 80s 2016 January	**In**	France New York Rugby Greenwich
Days/Weekends		**Streets/Roads**
Monday Saturday Thursday Friday	**On**	Broadway the M25 North Road Elm Street
Time		**Specific Location/Address**
7 o'clock 5:30 p.m. 13:20 half past 2	**At**	35 Acorn Grove Ahmed's house the stadium

daydream
EDUCATION

Conjunctions

Conjunctions are words that join two or more words, phrases, or clauses.

Coordinating Conjunctions

Coordinating conjunctions link together words, phrases and clauses that are of equal importance (such as two main clauses).

The acronym **FANBOYS** will help you remember the coordinating conjunctions.

| for | and | nor | but | or | yet | so |

I had fish and chips for tea.

You can order by phone or online.

Sophie says that she doesn't like dogs, yet she loves my puppy.

We are only away for one week, but it will be a week to remember.

Notice that a comma is needed when linking two main clauses.

Subordinating Conjunctions

Subordinating conjunctions are used in complex sentences to introduce subordinate clauses, (a clause that does not make sense on its own).

Here are some examples of subordinating conjunctions:

| because | if | where | before | while | however | when | despite |

When a subordinating conjunction is used **after a main clause**, a comma is not needed.

I will have to stop for a swim when I see the sea!

I need to remember to use sun cream before I go out.

When a subordinating conjunction is used at the **start of a sentence**, a comma is needed at the end of the subordinate clause.

Despite packing carefully, I still forgot my camera.

If we don't act now, we will lose the game.

Types of Sentences

Statements

A **statement** states a fact and ends with a full stop.

The school has a new playground.

It is raining again.

Ava's favourite sport is tennis.

Questions

A **question** asks for more information and ends with a question mark.

What time is it?

Where did you go on holiday?

Do you want to go shopping?

You can turn a statement into a question by adding a **question tag**:

You ate that apple I gave you, **didn't you?**

Commands

A **command** contains a command verb and can end with a full stop or exclamation mark.

Please **put your** homework on the desk.

Stop right there!

Tell me what happened in the film.

Exclamations

An **exclamation** expresses strong emotion and ends with an exclamation mark.

Don't do that!

What a goal!

The house is on fire!

daydream EDUCATIO

Sentences

When writing, you will need to use different sentences to suit your purpose, audience and text type. Use a variety of sentences to make your writing interesting and lively.

Minor Sentences

Minor sentences are very short, incomplete sentences:

 Stop!

 Hi!

 Go.

Simple Sentences

A simple sentence consists of only one clause, with a single **subject** and **predicate** (verb or verb phrase).

Simple sentences can contain multiple nouns, verbs, adjectives, adverbs, connectives and prepositions, but they cannot contain more than one clause.

I drove.

I drove slowly through the huge puddle.

Megan read.

Megan read her favourite actor's autobiography.

The dog barked and growled.

The fierce dog barked and growled loudly.

Compound Sentences

A compound sentence contains two or more main (independent) clauses that are linked by a coordinating conjunction (e.g. and, but, so, for, or).

The comedian told a joke, and the audience laughed uncontrollably.

It was hot and sunny, so we went to the beach.

Complex Sentences

A complex sentence contains a **main clause** and a subordinate clause. The subordinate clause supports the main clause and does not make sense on its own.

When he saw the first exam question, **he knew he was in trouble.**

Halle was late for school despite waking up early.

To make your writing more interesting, try to vary the types of sentences you use. Including adjectives, adverbs and imagery will also make your sentences more engaging.

Sentence Rules

A sentence is a group of words that are organised in a particular way so that they make sense.

If the words are not organised in the correct order, the sentence will not make sense.

✓ The boy ran down the street.

✗ The boy ran street the down.

Sentences start with a **capital letter** and end with a **full stop**.

It rained all day yesterday.	The dog barked loudly.	Football is my favourite sport.

Some sentences end with a **question mark** or **exclamation mark**. What time is it? Stop that now!

Almost every sentence needs a **verb** (a doing or being word) and a **subject**.

The snake hissed.	I feel sad.	Sophia rode her bike quickly.

Minor sentences usually do not have a definite verb. For sale. Help me!

The verb used in the sentence must be in the **correct tense and form**.

Simon built a shed. ✓	Simon builded a shed. ✗

We were eating dinner. ✓	We was eating dinner. ✗

I love my cat. ✓	I loves my cat. ✗

daydream
EDUCATION

Active and Passive Voice

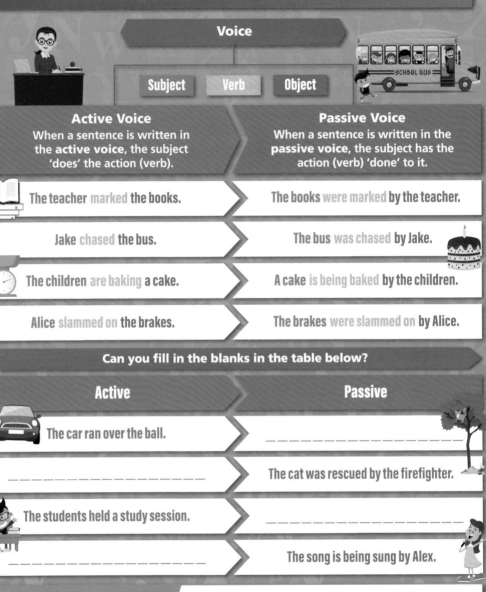

Voice

Subject | Verb | Object

Active Voice	Passive Voice
When a sentence is written in the **active voice**, the subject 'does' the action (verb).	When a sentence is written in the **passive voice**, the subject has the action (verb) 'done' to it.
The teacher marked the books.	The books were marked by the teacher.
Jake chased the bus.	The bus was chased by Jake.
The children are baking a cake.	A cake is being baked by the children.
Alice slammed on the brakes.	The brakes were slammed on by Alice.

Can you fill in the blanks in the table below?

Active	Passive
The car ran over the ball.	_____
_____	The cat was rescued by the firefighter.
The students held a study session.	_____
_____	The song is being sung by Alex.

Are the following sentences written in the active or passive voice?

Jamie and Ava were driven home by their parents.
The cake was eaten.
The wind blew off Priya's hat.

daydream EDUCATION

Phrases and Clauses

Phrases

A **phrase** is a group of words that form part of a clause or sentence.
It can contain nouns, adjectives, adverbs, prepositions and conjunctions.
However, it cannot contain both a subject and a verb.

Noun Phrase   **Conjunctival Phrase**

The children were playing basketball until it started to rain heavily.

The big, strong builder lifted the bricks with his bare hands.

Expanded Noun Phrase   **Adverbial Phrase**

Main Clauses

A **main clause** contains a **subject** and a **verb**. It makes sense on its own as a sentence.

Beth ate her dinner quickly.

My mum bought me a guitar.

The **car** broke down.

Two **main clauses**, of equal importance, can be joined using **coordinating conjunctions**.

I like Italian food, **but** Yousef likes Mexican food.

Zoe watched the film, **and** she read the book.

My alarm didn't go off, **so** I was late for work.

A comma is generally placed before the coordinating conjunction.

daydream EDUCATIO

Subordinate Clauses

A **subordinate clause** does not make sense on its own. It is introduced by a <u>subordinating conjunction</u>, and can be placed before or after the main clause.

I will go on the rollercoaster <u>although</u> I won't like it.

<u>Despite</u> being the better team, we didn't win.

Relative Clauses

A **relative clause** is a type of subordinate clause that describes, adapts or modifies a noun. Relative clauses begin with a <u>relative pronoun</u> and add more detail to sentences.

Relative Pronouns

who | whom | which | that | where | when | whose

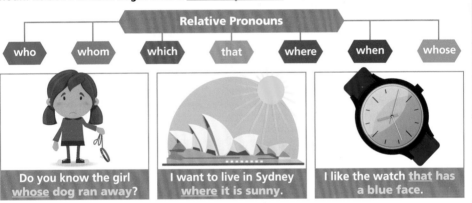

Do you know the girl <u>whose</u> dog ran away?

I want to live in Sydney <u>where</u> it is sunny.

I like the watch <u>that</u> has a blue face.

Embedded Clauses

An **embedded clause** is used in the middle of a main clause to add extra information. It is a type of subordinate clause.

The striker, who was very skilful, scored a great goal.

Paul, whose bike was broken, walked to school.

I left my coat, which is brand new, on the train.

An embedded clause is usually enclosed by commas.

Linking Words

Linking words, or cohesive devices, are words or phrases that are used to connect, organise and manage sentences.

Linking words can be used at the start, middle or end of sentences and paragraphs. However, they are often used as sentence or paragraph openers to help link ideas and create fluency. Below are some examples of linking words.

To add information

and   too   also   moreover   furthermore   as well as

The shopping centre is going to damage local businesses. **Furthermore**, it will cause traffic chaos.

To sequence events

firstly   secondly   after   before   next   meanwhile

Jack was frantically trying to finish his work. **Meanwhile**, his friends were at the party enjoying themselves.

To show similarities

likewise   also   similarly   equally   in the same way

Romeo falls into a deep depression. **Similarly**, Juliet despairs over the reality of her and Romeo's separation.

To contrast

whereas   however   on the other hand   conversely   alternatively

Aria enjoyed the film, **whereas** Mila thought it was boring.

To emphasise

especially   clearly   essentially   particularly   above all

Clearly, the politician was not comfortable with the question.

To show cause and effect

because   hence   therefore   as a result   consequently

Heena didn't get much sleep. **As a result**, she was unable to concentrate in her exam.

To conclude

in summary   overall   finally   in conclusion   to sum up

In summary, the phone was fit for purpose. However, it lacked key features that are available on other models.

To illustrate

for example   such as   including   according to   for instance

I like citrus fruits, **such as** oranges, lemons and satsumas.

Can you think of any other linking words?

 daydream
EDUCATION

Standard English

Standard English	The form of the English language that is widely accepted as the correct form.
Dialect	A form of the language that is different to the standard and is specific to a region or social group.
Slang	Informal (non-standard) words or phrases that are often specific to a particular group.

Standard English is used by the majority of people. However, there are variations in spelling and grammar between many spoken dialects and standard English.

Non-standard English	Rule	Standard English
We was at the park. ✗ I knows the answer. ✗	There must be subject-verb agreement.	✓ We were at the park. ✓ I know the answer.
I seen the film. ✗ Abby done it wrong. ✗	Verbs must be written in the correct tense.	✓ I saw the film. ✓ Abby did it wrong.
We didn't see nobody. ✗ I never took nothing. ✗	Do not use double negatives.	✓ We didn't see anyone. ✓ I never took anything.
I should of gone. ✗ You could of won. ✗	Do not use 'of' instead of 'have'.	✓ I should have gone. ✓ You could have won.

Slang

Do not use slang in your writing, unless you are quoting direct speech.

bae	ain't	gutted	swag
geet	chuffed	owt	dunno

Paragraphs

A paragraph is a group of related sentences that focus on a specific theme or topic.

Change of Topic

A new paragraph is needed when there is a new topic, development **or** idea.

He had begun to despair when he saw the keys. They were lying on the floor. They had been shaken out of the greatcoat pocket when the guard fell. Quickly Joseph fished for the ring of keys and hauled it up.

> Here there is a change of topic from Joseph's feelings about the keys (he needed to escape) to his actions.

Change of Time

A new paragraph is needed when there is a change in time.

During the summer his health mended, but the number of guards was doubled. A group of six - he was one of them - tried to break away together, but the attempt failed. For this he had a month of solitary confinement.

The following winter he was ill again, but no less determined to escape. He decided to wait till early spring, when the snow was beginning to melt and the nights were not so bitter.

Change of Speaker

A new paragraph is needed when there is a change of speaker.

Ruth's family was in one of the open trucks, which was cold but not quite so crowded.

"I don't like this truck," said Bronia "It jolts too much."

"Every jolt takes us nearer to Switzerland," said Ruth.

"Think of it like that and it's not so bad."

"There's no room to stretch."

"Rest your head against me and try and go to sleep. There, that's better."

Change of Person or Place

A new paragraph is needed when a new person or place is introduced.

It was the end of May when the train reached Berlin - after nine days of stopping and starting, of lying up in sidings, of crawling along the battered track.

The station was a shambles, but everyone was glad to escape from their cramped quarters. They swarmed out of the trucks and over the lines, some of them disappearing at once into the dusty ruins of Berlin.

All extracts taken from 'The Silver Sword' by Ian Serraillier.

Capital Letters — and when to use them.

Starting a Sentence

Every sentence starts with a **capital letter**.

A long time ago, in a galaxy far, far away...

A capital letter is usually required at the start of direct speech.

"Stop that man!" shouted the police officer.

Names and Titles

Sarah took her son to see **D**r. **W**illiams because he was ill.

Days of the Week and Months

The football game is on **M**onday 2nd **J**uly.

Place Names

I'm moving to **S**ydney, **A**ustralia.

Nationalities and Languages

The man is **M**exican but he speaks **S**panish.

"Hola!"

Companies and Organisations

The **RSPCA** takes care of injured and abandoned animals.

Headings and Book/Film Titles

My favourite book is **A**lice in **W**onderland.

Punctuation

Full Stop

A full stop marks the end of a sentence.

Josephine had to push her bike all the way home. The front tyre had a puncture and was completely flat.

Comma

A comma separates items in a list. It is also used to punctuate speech and separate parts of a sentence, such as clauses, to help clarify meaning.

The bag contained trainers, shorts, a shirt, socks and a water bottle.

Let's eat Grandma.

Let's eat, Grandma.

Question Mark

A question mark indicates the end of a question.

What is your name?

Do you know when to use a question mark?

Exclamation Mark

An exclamation mark is used to end a dramatic sentence or statement.

Don't put your hand in the fire!

Look out!

Speech Marks

Speech marks, or inverted commas, indicate direct speech, i.e. the exact words spoken.

"I like football," said Sam.
"Me too," replied Ella.
"Which team do you support?"

daydream
EDUCATI

Colon

A colon introduces extra information, such as a list. It connects parts of a sentence, where the second part provides further explanation of the first.

George thought it was his mum's fault: she shouldn't have moved his homework when she was tidying up.

Semi-Colon

A semi-colon links two clauses of equal importance. It is also used to separate items in a list, when the list already contains commas.

The expedition may be on or off; it all depends on the weather. The guides are: Sam Yates, Biology; Amy Eliot, Physics; and Julie Cooper, Chemistry.

Apostrophe

An apostrophe is used to show ownership or that a letter is missing.

The rabbit's tail is black. (The tail belongs to the rabbit.)

It is going to rain.
↓
It's going to rain.

Brackets

Brackets are used to indicate parenthesis – extra information that is separate from the main sentence or statement.

Dashes (see below) can also be used to separate extra information.

Dashes

Dashes are also used to indicate parenthesis – extra information that is separate from the main sentence or statement. They are twice the length of a hyphen.

All of the ingredients – tomatoes, basil, onion, garlic and chilli – were ready for cooking.

Hyphen

A hyphen is used to join words together. It can join prefixes to root words, and words that are linked, such as compound adjectives.

She is an award-winning novelist.

Commas

Commas can make your writing clear and easy to read. However, if used incorrectly, or not at all, they can make your writing confusing and inaccurate.

Separating Items in a List

Commas are used to separate items in a list when there are three or more items. A list that doesn't contain commas is often difficult to understand.

I bought a t-shirt skirt jumper and two pairs of shoes.   I bought a t-shirt, skirt, jumper and two pairs of shoes.

The politician vowed to lower taxes increase wages and reduce crime.   The politician vowed to lower taxes, increase wages and reduce crime.

A comma is not usually used before the last item, unless it is needed for clarification.

The café sells three types of sandwich: ham and salad, chicken and bacon, and cheese.

Separating Clauses and Extra Information

Commas are used to break up a sentence to clarify meaning.

A comma can be used to **separate subordinate clauses and non-essential information** from the main point in a sentence.

The soldiers, **led by Sergeant Rowan,** planned a revolt.
One of the soldiers refused to help, **which caused a problem.**

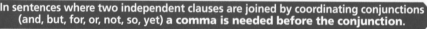
In sentences where two independent clauses are joined by coordinating conjunctions (and, but, for, or, not, so, yet) **a comma is needed before the conjunction.**

I want to live in Paris, **so** I am studying French at A-level.

I read the instructions, **but** they were not very helpful.

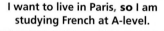
If there is an introductory clause, phrase or word before the main clause, a comma is needed after the introductory clause.

Last Sunday, we went to a music festival.

Traditionally, shops have only stayed open late on a Thursday night.

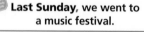
Commas are also used in **names, dates, numbers** and **geographical names.**

His son, **Mark Smith,** was born on **December 19, 2014,** in **London, England.**

daydream
EDUCATE

Separating Adjectives

A comma is used to separate adjectives when the order of the adjectives is interchangeable.

The strong, agile striker beat the defender.

The agile, strong striker beat the defender.

This rule does not apply when the adjectives are not interchangeable.

They went to an expensive summer resort.

No comma needed, as the order of the adjectives cannot be swapped:

They went to a summer, expensive resort.

Punctuating Speech

A comma is used to introduce speech and when the sentence continues after the speech:

Max protested, "It wasn't my fault!" "Tell me what happened," said the police officer.

Comma Splicing

Two sentences, or independent clauses, cannot be linked just using a comma. You can fix a comma splice by:

I looked at my shoes, they were filthy.

Making two sentences

I looked at my shoes. They were filthy.

Harry has finished his essay, he hasn't submitted it.

Adding a conjunction

Harry has finished his essay, **but** he hasn't submitted it.

Jess calls it football, Luciano calls it soccer.

Using a semi-colon

Jess calls it football; Luciano calls it soccer.

Commas can be used wherever necessary to prevent confusion. Look at how the following sentences are similar but have completely different meanings!

Let's eat Grandma!

Let's eat, Grandma!

Don't stop!

Don't, stop!

The Apostrophe

Apostrophes are used either to show ownership or to show a letter is missing.

Possession

In speech we add an **s** to show **possession** or **ownership**.
In written English, we also add an **apostrophe**.

Singular Possession

When showing ownership by one person or subject, an **apostrophe** and an **s** are added.

The cat's tail is black.

The man's hat is yellow.

The shop's sign is broken.

Aisha's homework was late.

Plural Possession

When showing ownership by more than one person or subject, two different rules apply:

When a word already ends in **s**, only add an **apostrophe**.

 The cats' tails are black.

 Their parents' house was huge.

 He found two suspects' DNA.

When a word does not end in **s**, add an **apostrophe** and an **s**.

 The men's hats are yellow.

 The children's school is closed.

 The media's coverage was biased.

When showing ownership by more than one person or subject in a list, only add an **apostrophe** and an **s** to the last mentioned person or subject.

 Sophie, Ben and Maya's dog had to go to the vet.

You do **not** need to add an apostrophe to pronouns such as:

its **whose** **yours** **his** **hers** **ours** **theirs**

daydrea
EDUCAT

Missing Letters

An apostrophe can be used to indicate that letters have been missed out.

Do not get dirty.	Don't get dirty.
Where is the map?	Where's the map?
I am taller than my brother.	I'm taller than my brother.
Anna does not need her gloves.	Anna doesn't need her gloves.
To catch the train, she would have to get up at 6 o'clock.	To catch the train, she'd have to get up at 6 o'clock.

Common Mistakes

It's = It is It's time to go home.	It's or Its	Its = possessive pronoun Its tail is very long.
You're = You are You're going to be late.	You're or Your	Your = possessive pronoun Your coat is too small.
Who's = Who is Do you know who's coming to the party?	Who's or Whose	Whose = possessive pronoun Whose house is that?
We're = We are We're the best team in the league.	We're or Were	Were = verb You were at the shops.

Can you complete the following sentences?

It's or Its	We're or Were	You're or Your
_____ a long way to the train station.	Who knows where _____ going?	_____ rugby kit is in the wash.

Remember, do **not** use an apostrophe to make a plural:	CD's will soon be obsolete, just like video's. ✗ CDs will soon be obsolete, just like videos. ✓

Direct Speech

There are several rules that need to be followed when quoting direct speech (spoken words).

		Explanation	Example
1	**Speech Marks**	Speech marks, or inverted commas, are used to indicate direct speech. They enclose the spoken words.	"What do you want to do this weekend?" asked Abby.
2	**Exact Words**	Only use speech marks when quoting the exact spoken words. Indirect speech does not need speech marks.	Abby asked us what we wanted to do this weekend. ✗ no speech marks needed
3	**Capital Letters**	Use a capital letter at the start of direct speech, **unless the speech is a continuation of an existing sentence.**	"Stay there!" he shouted. "You can't leave now!" "We are going to France," he said, "**but** not until March."
4	**Punctuation** (inside speech marks)	Place any punctuation that belongs to the direct speech inside the speech marks.	"When are we having lunch?" asked Toby. "Get out!" shouted the teacher.
5	**Punctuation** (outside speech marks)	Place any punctuation that does not belong to the direct speech outside the speech marks.	Did Arnold really say, "I'll be back"?
6	**Commas**	Use a comma if the text continues after the direct speech. You also need to use a comma when introducing direct speech.	"That's an iconic movie quote," said Mike. Beth replied, "Yes, I know."
7	**New Paragraphs**	Start a new paragraph every time there is a new speaker.	"Do you like apples?" asked Will. "I always wondered." "Yes. Why do you ask?" replied Tomek.

daydrea EDUCAT

Word Building

Root (base) words are words in the simplest form. You can make root words longer and change their meaning by adding prefixes and/or suffixes.

Prefix	Root (base) word	Suffix
Prefixes are added to the beginning of root words to change their meaning.	**Root words** are complete words that make sense on their own.	**Suffixes** are added to the end of root words to change their meaning.

dis	joint	ed
un	**friend**	**ly**
il	**logic**	**al**

Prefixes

Prefixes change the meaning of a root word.
However, the spelling of the root word never changes.

unfriendly

The above prefix reverses the meaning of the root word.

redirect

The above prefix changes the meaning of the root word.

Diversion

Suffixes

Suffixes can change the meaning, tense or class of root words. They can also be used to make singular root words plural.

Tense	jog ⟶ **jog**ged	
Class	**begin** (verb) ⟶ **beginning** (noun)	
Plural	carry ⟶ **carr**ied	
Meaning	care ⟶ **care**less	

Notice how the addition of a suffix can change the spelling of the root word.

Common Prefixes

Meaning 'not'

The following prefixes mean **not** and reverse the meaning of the root word.

legal **il** **il**legal

regular **ir** **ir**regular

happy **un** **un**happy

appear **dis** **dis**appear

active **in** **in**active

polite **im** **im**polite

Adelle's mum was **un**happy and **dis**approved of the shop assistant's **im**polite manner.

Meaning 'physically below' or 'of lesser importance'

The following prefixes mean **physically below** or **of lesser importance**.

undercover

understudy

subway

subplot

Florence, Lilly's **under**study, caught the **sub**way to the theatre.

Other Prefixes

mis – incorrect or bad

misspell

re – again

replay

pre – before

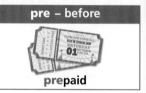
prepaid

super – excessive

superstar

bi – two

bicycle

post – after

postgame

daydrea EDUCA

Common Suffixes

Change of Tense

Suffixes are often used to change the **tense** of the root word.

pass pass**ed** call call**ed** carry carr**ied**

Notice how the spelling of the root word 'carry' has changed.

Change from Singular to Plural

Suffixes are often used to change the root word from **singular** to **plural**.

crutch crutch**es** car car**s** lady lad**ies**

Notice how the spelling of the root word 'lady' has changed.

Change of Word Class

Suffixes are often used to change the **class** of the root word.

quick  quick**ly**
(adjective) ▶ (adverb)

wonder **ful** wonder**ful**
(noun) ▶ (adjective)

celebrate **ion** celebrat**ion**
(verb) ▶ (noun)

Other Examples

Although suffixes do not make sense on their own, they do have particular meanings.

The suffix **ful** means **full of**.

The power**ful** car sped away.

The suffixes **ful** and **less** have opposite meanings.

The suffix **less** means **without**.

The waiter was care**less**.

The suffix **er** is used to compare things, or to describe a person in terms of his/her occupation or hobby.

The sprint**er** can run fast**er** than her rivals.

sense sens**ible**

love lov**able**

ambition ambi**tious**

grace **cious** gra**cious**

office **cial** offi**cial**

influence **tial** influen**tial**

daydream
EDUCATION

Plurals

Plural means more than one.

Adding 's'

Most plurals are formed by simply adding s.

book ▶ books

dog ▶ dogs

bottle ▶ bottles

Adding 'es'

When a word ends in s, x, sh or ch we add es to make it plural.

glass ▶ glasses

box ▶ boxes

dish ▶ dishes

watch ▶ watches

Ending in f or fe

Replace the f or fe with ves to make it plural.

leaf ▶ leaves

knife ▶ knives

Ending in y

If there is a vowel before the y, add s to make it plural.

monkey ▶ monkeys

If there is a consonant before the y, replace it with ies to make it plural.

berry ▶ berries

Ending in o

If there is a vowel before the o, add s to make it plural.

kangaroo ▶ kangaroos

If there is a consonant before the o, add es to make it plural.

tomato ▶ tomatoes

Irregular Plurals

Plurals that do not follow a spelling rule are called irregular plurals.

sheep - sheep

foot - feet

fungus - fungi

34

daydrea EDUCA

Tricky Spellings

Silent Letters

Some words contain silent letters that are not sounded out when they are said.

K	B	W	T	H
knight	lamb	wrong	castle	honest
knee	climb	sword	thistle	when
knife	doubt	write	ballet	ghost

Other words that contain silent letters include:

island   solemn   design   build   gnome   column

Can you think of any others?

Letter String Ough

The letter string **ough** is used in many words to represent different word sounds.

aw	uff	oh
bought	tough	though
fought	rough	dough
thought	enough	although

ow	off	oo
drought	cough	through
plough	trough	throughout

Unstressed and Stressed Vowels

Some words contain unstressed vowels that are not easily heard when they are said.

Isaac was interested in the different pieces of jewellery that he saw in the museum.

The fer spelling rule

When adding a suffix to a word ending in **fer**, you double the r if the fer is still stressed after the suffix is added:	refer ▶ referred transfer ▶ transferred
If the **fer** is unstressed, you do not need to double the r:	prefer ▶ preference

daydream EDUCATION

i Before e?

The rule is easy to remember: i before e except after c (but only when it rhymes with bee).

Rhymes with 'bee'

- The **ie** in these examples rhymes with 'bee'.
- There is no **c**, so the **i** comes **before** the **e**.

Other examples: field, handkerchief.

thief   **chief**

- The **ei** in these examples rhymes with 'bee'.
- There is a **c**, so the **i** comes **after** the **e**.

Other examples: receipt, perceive.

receive   **deceive**

Doesn't rhyme with 'bee'

- The **ie** in these examples doesn't rhyme with 'bee'.
- There is a **c**, so the **i** comes **before** the **e**.

Other examples: efficient, sufficient.

scientist   **ancient**

- The **ei** in these examples doesn't rhyme with 'bee'.
- There is no **c**, so the **i** comes **after** the **e**.

Other examples: freight, height.

eight   **weight**

Here are some exceptions to the rule: **weird** | **seize** | **neighbour**

daydrea EDUCAT

To, Two and Too

To, two and too are homophones: words that sound the same but have different spellings and meanings.

To

To is often used with a destination or a verb.

I want to pass my maths exam.

Max went on holiday to Spain.

Luca isn't speaking to his sister.

Two

Two is the number 2.

Olivia can speak two languages.

I ate two pieces of fruit this morning.

There were two accidents on the motorway.

Too

Too is used to mean as well or excessively.

Emma wanted a coffee too.

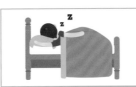

I was too tired to go training last night.

Bailey's boots are too big.

Can you complete the following sentences?

I wanted _____ buy _____ new dresses but they were _____ expensive.

Mia's food was _____ hot _____ eat.

Logan went _____ the shops and bought _____ chocolate bars.

daydream
EDUCATION

There, Their, They're

There, their and they're are homophones: words that sound the same but have different spellings and meanings.

There

There is used with the words 'is', 'are', 'was' and 'were' to indicate that something exists (or doesn't exist). It can also be used to refer to a place.

There is my house.

The three firemen are over there.

There are no leaves on the trees.

Their

Their is used to show possession by more than one person or thing.

They played with their football.

Their mum was very angry.

They lost their concert tickets.

They're

They're is the shortened form of 'they are'.

They are at the cinema with their friends so I am sure they are having a good time.

They're at the cinema with their friends so I am sure they're having a good time.

CINEMA

To check that you are using the correct word, actually say 'they are' in your sentence.

Can you complete the following sentences?

_____ going to the cinema to watch _____ favourite film.

_____ are 30 people in the queue and _____ all fed up.

_____ is a big swimming pool in _____ hotel.

daydream
EDUCAT

Your and You're

Your and **you're** are homophones: words that sound the same but have different spellings and meanings.

Your

Your is used to show **possession** or **belonging**.

Your dinner is ready.

Your boots are in your bag.

I think your battery is low.

Where have you parked your car?

You're

You're is the shortened form of **you are**.

You're going to be late.

I'm glad you're my brother.

You're a better driver than me.

You're not funny.

To check that you're using the correct word, actually say **'you are'** in your sentence.

Examples

Your spaghetti is the best. ✓	✗	You're spaghetti is the best.
Your amazing on the guitar. ✗	✓	You're amazing on the guitar.
What is your dog's name? ✓	✗	What is you're dog's name?

Can you complete the following sentences?

Dear Molly, I hope _____ well.

Tell _____ manager that _____ going to be late.

_____ crazy!

Know, Now and No

Know, now and no are words that are commonly mixed up.

Know

Know means to be familiar with someone or something.

I know why the sky is blue.

Do you know how to play the guitar?

Alex knows that you ate the last chocolate bar.

Now

Now is used to refer to the present time or moment.

I want to go home now.

If he doesn't go now, he will be late.

You are now old enough to drive.

No

No is used as a negative response or to mean none or not any.

No, thank you. I don't like sweets.

There were no bargains in the sale.

The hotel has no vacancies.

Can you complete the following sentences?

_____, I don't _____ where the remote is.

Do you _____ the difference between them _____ ?

Can we go shopping _____ ?

daydrea EDUCAT

Synonyms & Antonyms

Synonyms are words that have the same or a very similar meaning. They are used to avoid repeating the same word and can make your writing more interesting.

The happy clown waved to the happy children.

joyful   merry   cheerful

The following are examples of synonyms:

hilarious	dash	angry	thief
funny	run	annoyed	robber
comical	jog	irritated	burglar

Antonyms

Antonyms are words that have opposite meanings.

big **or** small

weak **or** strong

wet **or** dry

light **or** dark

You can create some antonyms by adding a negative prefix to the word:

happy ▶ un**happy**   agree ▶ dis**agree**   complete ▶ in**complete**

A thesaurus is a book that lists words in groups of synonyms and related concepts. They will also often include antonyms.

Homophones

Homophones are words that sound the same but have different spellings and meanings. As a result, they are commonly mixed up.

pair or **pear**

weak or **week**

break or **brake**

peace or **piece**

tale or **tail**

see or **sea**

Passed is the past tense of the verb 'to pass'.

He passed his driving test.

passed or past

Past means 'time before the present', or 'beyond'.

Don't go past the tape.

'Practice' is a noun.

Swimming practice starts at 8 o'clock.

practice or practise

'Practise' is a verb.

She likes to practise her swimming before school.

Near Homophones

Some words that look and sound similar are also commonly mixed up...

quiet or **quite**

device or **devise**

accept or **except**

'Effect' means 'the result of something'.

The effects of the accident were devastating.

effect or affect

'Affect' means 'to influence something'.

Poor grammar affects your credibility.

'Advice' is a noun.

Let me give you some advice.

advice or advise

'Advise' is a verb.

I advise you to follow the instructions.

Homonyms

Homonyms are words that are spelt and sound the same but have different meanings.

Book the room that you saw in the **book**.

Watch where you put your **watch**.

daydrea EDUCAT

Reading Skills

lose Reading ▶ Reading and rereading the text carefully to determine its meaning; often involves annotating or highlighting key points and supporting evidence

kimming ▶ Reading the text quickly to identify overall meaning

canning ▶ Reading the text quickly to locate specific information

Reading and Responding to Questions

To answer any question, you need to understand exactly what it is asking. Read the questions properly, highlighting or **underlining** the keywords.

Write a summary of the differences between Chris and Zoe.

Questions will often ask you different things...

Locate and Retrieve

ome questions expect you to find key details. To do this, scan the text for the keywords that are relevant to the question.

According to the text, how did the weather affect pupils' behaviour?

Make Comparisons

Some questions will ask you to gather information from different texts and make comparisons. Find similarities and differences to give a balanced answer.

Compare how Jamie and Chloe feel about moving house.

Evaluate and Explain

ometimes you will be asked to explain or make judgements about something in a text, such as the writer's opinion or the language used in the text.

How has the writer used imagery to influence the reader?

Infer

Some questions expect you to work out the answer even though it is not stated directly in the text. Use clues and hints in the text to 'read between the lines'.

How do you think the writer would react to the following statement?

Summarise

You may be asked to summarise or outline the main points of a text. To do this, skim the text to find the main points to create a concise overview.

What is the writer's opinion on dog licensing?

Predict

Sometimes you will be asked to make predictions. Don't just guess – look at what has already happened for clues and evidence to support your answer.

What does this extract suggest might happen next?

daydream EDUCATION

43

Point, Evidence, Explain

The **Point, Evidence, Explain** technique can be used when writing and answering questions. State your point of view, back it up with evidence and then explain it.

P Point — State your main point.

E Evidence — Provide evidence to support your point.

E Explain — Explain the evidence in more detail and how it supports your point.

Examples

What do newspaper editors use in their headlines to attract attention?

P Newspaper editors use puns to grab people's attention.
E For example, this newspaper's headline states, 'He Must
E Be Parking Mad!'. This is a play on words, as it replaces 'barking' with 'parking'. Puns often use humour to attract people's attention.

How does the advert try to persuade people to buy the product?

P The advert uses persuasive techniques to try to convince
E people to buy the product. It uses statistics – '99% of
E people agree it's the best' – to make readers feel assured that they can trust the product.

What is your first impression of Ebenezer Scrooge?

P Ebenezer Scrooge is a bitter, miserable old man. For example, when
E his nephew visits him and wishes him a merry Christmas, he responds by saying, 'Every idiot who goes about with "Merry Christmas" on his lips, should be boiled with his own pudding, and
E buried with a stake of holly through his heart.' This statement shows that Ebenezer Scrooge is rude and very unpleasant as he turns the image of Christmas into images of violence.

daydrea
EDUCAT

Fact vs Opinion

When reading a text, it is important to know the difference between fact and opinion.

Fact

A **fact** is a true statement that can be proven through research or observations.

numbers
statistics
measures
times & dates
scientific data
names
historical events

Opinion

An **opinion** is a personal view or judgement that cannot be proven.

descriptive words
thoughts
feelings
might
believe
should
think
point of view

Fact	Opinion
Nelson Mandela was born on 18th July 1918.	Nelson Mandela was the best president of South Africa.
The average temperature in London in July is 19°C.	The weather in London in July is pleasant.
Earth is the third planet from the sun.	I think there is life on other planets in the solar system.
Bananas are yellow.	Bananas taste nice.
This year, 10% more pupils had detention than last year.	The behaviour of pupils is getting worse.

Be careful, opinions are sometimes expressed as if they are facts. Therefore, always check the reliability of statements or claims.

☑ Can the information be checked through research?
☑ Is there supporting evidence?
☑ Does the statement express a fact, feeling or belief?

A writer may use a combination of fact and opinion to influence the reader. Remember, facts are always true, whereas opinions are disputable.

45

Purpose, Audience, Form

Before writing a text, it is important to identify its purpose, your audience and the required form. This will help you choose what language and structure to use in your writing.

Purpose

It is vital that you achieve your purpose. Think "Why am I writing?"

Argue/Persuade

Describe

Entertain

Inform, Explain, Advise

Instruct

❓ Can you think of any other purposes? ❓

The purpose of your text will affect the language and structure you use. For example, the language and structure used in a persuasive advert is completely different to that used in a formal letter.

Audience

You must tailor your writing to suit your audience. Think "Who am I writing to?" How would you change your writing for each of the following audiences?

Friends

Children

Potential Employers

Politicians

The nature of your audience will have a big impact on the language and tone you use in your writing. For example, the language used in an article for a children's magazine will be different to that used in a scientific journal.

Form (text type)

Your writing needs to be presented in a suitable form. Think "How am I going to present and structure my writing?" You will often be asked to write a specific type of text.

Newspaper Article

Letter

Diary

Advert

Presentation

Blog

Review

Report

Remember to think about how P.A.F. changes the way you write. However, always ensure that your spelling, punctuation and grammar are correct.

daydrea EDUCATE

Planning, Organising & Writing

Planning

Once you know your purpose, format and audience, you can start to create a plan. Use spider diagrams or bullet points to create a list of your main ideas or key points.

- All Stars vs Athletico, FS Cup Final, Paris Stadium, 12th September 2016.
- Mossi scores a brilliant free kick for Athletico on 14 min.
- **My Match Report**
- Referee wrongly awards All Stars a penalty on 34 min but Beal misses.
- Athletico win 1-0 despite All Stars having 65% of the possession.
- Keane sent off for All Stars on 84 min for diving.

Organising

Once you have outlined the key points, organise your ideas in a logical order.

Remember to include key features for the text type you're writing.

Writing

- ☑ Remember your purpose and intended audience.
- ☑ Follow your plan and stick to the subject.
- ☑ Use paragraphs to structure and organise your writing.
- ☑ Use accurate spelling, punctuation and grammar.
- ☑ Use a wide range of vocabulary.
- ☑ Use interesting adverbs and adjectives.

Format:
Newspaper report

Headline:
Athleticooooooohhhh!

Basic information:
FS Cup Final, Paris Stadium, 12th September 2016. Athletico FC become world champions after beating valiant opponents, All Stars, 1-0 in a thrilling contest.

Explanation (further detail):
1. After a cagey start from both teams, Mossi scored a thrilling free kick on 14 minutes to put Athletico up 1-0.

2. Then, on 34 minutes, Beal missed a penalty for All Stars.

3. In the second half, All Stars tried too hard, and Keane was sent off on 84 minutes for a terrible dive.

4. Upon the final whistle, there were scenes of jubilation amongst the Athletico fans and players.

5. All Stars' manager was not happy after the game, stating that his team "lacked skill and intelligence".

Close:
Despite dominating the game, All Stars did not create any real chances, and Athletico were deserved winners.

Proofreading Checklist

With any piece of writing, it is vital to **plan** and **proofread** your work.
Use the checklist below to ensure that your work is correct and fit for purpose.

Capitalisation

☑ Do all sentences start with a capital letter?
☑ Have you used capital letters for names and titles, days and months, place names, nationalities, languages and headings?

Joseph grew up in Paris, so he is fluent in French. ✓

Bonjour!

Organisation

☑ Do all sentences make sense: are the words in the correct order?
☑ Could you change any sentences to make them easier to understand?
☑ Have you used a variety of sentence structures?
☑ Is there verb-subject agreement within your sentences?

Amelia done a great job. ✗   Amelia did a great job. ✓

Punctuation

☑ Do all of your sentences end with the correct punctuation mark?
☑ Have you used apostrophes correctly?

Remember not to use commas to separate two independent clauses!

I looked outside,
it was raining. ✗

I looked outside.
It was raining. ✓

Spelling

☑ Have you checked the spelling of words that you are unsure of?
☑ Have you used the correct homophone?

I hope your well. ✗   I hope you're well. ✓

Remember not to use slang or text speak.

Paragraphs

☑ Have you separated your writing into paragraphs?
☑ Have you used a new paragraph whenever there is a change in: topic, time, speaker, person or place?

For this he had a month of solitary confinement.
   The following winter he was ill again, but no less determined to escape. He decided to wait till early s

48

daydream
EDUCATI

Vocabulary

☑ If writing poetry or a creative text, have you used imagery and a variety of adjectives, verbs and adverbs?

Tyrion looked into her eyes.

Tyrion gazed, mesmerized, into her deep blue eyes that sparkled like ice cubes in a thirst-quenching summer drink.

☑ If analysing, have you used quotes to back up your opinion, and subject terminology to demonstrate your knowledge?

Romeo uses a simile to exaggerate Juliet's beauty:

"The brightness of her cheek would shame those stars, as daylight doth a lamp."

Form

☑ Does your text include the relevant features for its form?

Adverts	Articles	Creative Writing
Persuasive language, direct address, emotive language	Quotes, facts, headlines, subheadings	Imagery and descriptive language

Correcting Mistakes

Neatly cross out errors and write the correction above.
Do not write over the error or cross out individual letters.

In the artic~~la~~, Mr. Sullivan gives his personal opinion on the budget.

article
In the ~~artical~~, Mr. Sullivan gives his personal opinion on the budget.

If you have missed something out, insert a '^' and write the additional text above.

walked
Chloe tentatively ^ through the tiny passage.

If there is not enough room, insert an asterisk (*) where the text needs to be added and write the missing words at the end of your text with another asterisk before.

Both poems investigate the theme of the weather.*The writers use metaphors and personification to portray the harshness of the weather.

However, poem A looks at the brutality of winter, while poem B investigates the power of the sun.

Summarising Texts

To summarise a text, find the most important points and rewrite them in your own words, in a shortened form.

1
Read the question and identify exactly what it is asking for.

A question will not just ask you to summarise the whole text. It will ask for specific details.

Underline or highlight the keywords in the question to identify exactly what needs to be summarised.

Write a summary of the **differences between Chris and Zoe.**

2
Read the original text to identify its overall meaning.

The meaning of a text is not usually mentioned directly. Therefore, to understand the meaning of the text you will need to consider its purpose and the language, tone and structure used by the writer.

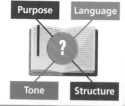

Purpose   Language   Tone   Structure

3
Locate the key points in the text.

A summary is a shortened form of a longer piece of text. Therefore, it should only contain the main points.

Locate and highlight the key information, ignoring any minor details. Creating a table of the key points may help.

4
Write the summary in your own words.

Write the summary in your own words, but use quotes and extracts from the original text to support your answer.

Do not give your own opinion; only include the facts. Link together your sentences and paragraphs using conjunctions.

Chris is a typical teenager. He speaks to his father in a 'sarcastic tone'. In contrast, Zoe is very formal with her father addressing him respectfully as 'my dear father'.

5
Check your summary.

Check that your summary has maintained the overall purpose and meaning of the original text.

As with all text types, remember to proofread your summary to ensure it is free from spelling, punctuation and grammatical errors.

PROOFREAD
- ✓ SPELLING
- ✓ PUNCTUATION
- ✓ GRAMMAR

daydream
EDUCATI

Explanations

Explanations provide detailed descriptions about how something works or why something happens.

Explanations can be quite complicated, so it is important to plan out what you are going to write about. Think about:

| What you are explaining and why | The order in which things happen | The audience and how it affects the language and format you use |

How to Keep a New Plant Healthy

Heading: clearly state what is going to be explained.

Many pupils are now involved in looking after their school gardens. Not only is this useful for when they grow up and have their own gardens, but it encourages interaction with nature and wildlife. In order for a garden to flourish, it is vital to know how to take care of a variety of plants.

Introduction: explain what you are writing about and why.

First, a plant should be planted at the right time of year. If it is planted in the winter, it is not likely to survive because of exposure to frost. Additionally, ensure that the plant's roots are kept moist.

A plant should only be placed in earth that will allow it to grow. For example, soil rich in lime can inhibit growth. Secondly, it is essential that the plant gets sufficient light. Some plants require lots of sunshine, whilst others can survive in the shade, so it is important to research what is best for the plants you are using.

Use devices such as conjunctions and adverbials to build cohesion and link ideas.

If needed, include diagrams to help explain difficult points.

Before planting, dig a hole that is deeper and wider than the roots, and fill it with water and natural fertiliser. Next, carefully place the roots in the hole, which can then be filled with the displaced earth.

Write in the present tense.

In the days and weeks that follow, a watchful eye is needed to ensure the plant remains healthy. It must be watered regularly, especially when it is hot and dry.

Use interesting facts to engage the reader.

The best nurtured gardens are those in which plants have been carefully rooted and nurtured.

Explain any technical terminology, possibly in a glossary of terms.

Formal Letter

A formal letter is used when you write to someone you do not know or the content is impersonal.

Examples include job applications and business letters. Plan out your letter and ask yourself:

Why am I writing this letter?

Who is my audience?

What response do I want?

The name and address of the person to whom you are writing.

Your full address → 6 Cherry Lane
Maple Town
AB1 2CD

Date → 21st July 2016

Greeting: Use the title and name of the person to whom you are writing.

Mr. D. Taylor
Taylor Games
Unit 1, North Avenue
Brick Town
WX1 2YZ

Reference: The heading of your letter. It tells the reader what the letter is about.

Dear Mr. Taylor,

Re: Customer Service Complaint, Order Number 20340506

Opening paragraph:
Explain why you are writing the letter. Be clear and to the point.

I am writing to complain about the awful customer service that I received from your company over the last six weeks in relation to my order.

I purchased a computer game on the 5th June, on a guaranteed five-day delivery service, allowing plenty of time for delivery before my son's birthday in July.

Main paragraphs:
Explain what has happened in more detail.

Do not write one large paragraph. Use connectives or write a paragraph for each point.

Support opinions with facts.

After ten days, the game still hadn't arrived so I sent an email to find out where it was. Two days later, there was still no response, so I tried to contact you by phone. However, I was only able to get through to an answer phone message.

On the 26th June, I finally spoke to one of your customer services representatives, who assured me that my order had finally been dispatched and would be delivered on the 2nd July, just in time for my son's birthday.

Much to my disappointment, six weeks after placing my order, I am still waiting for the computer game to arrive. The issue has caused an enormous disruption and is not something that I expected from a reputable online retailer.

I am offended by the lack of respect shown by your company and demand that a refund be issued immediately.

I look forward to hearing from you.

Yours sincerely,

Conclusion:
Repeat the main point and explain what response or outcome you want.

Close: Use 'Yours sincerely' if you know the name of the person to whom you are writing. If not, use 'Yours faithfully'.

S. Williams

Your signature and name.

Ms. Sarah Williams

Remember: Always reread and check your letter before sending!

daydream
EDUCATI

Informal Letter

An informal letter is used when writing to a friend or family member. As a result, it can be relaxed, familiar and friendly.

There is no need to include the address of the person to whom you are writing.

Greeting: You can use the person's first name in an informal letter.

Opening paragraph: include a greeting and explain why you are writing. Use relaxed and friendly language as you know the person to whom you are writing.

Main paragraphs: Explain what has happened in more detail. Do not write one large paragraph. Use connectives or write a paragraph for each point. Support opinions with facts.

Using connectives will help your letter flow.

How you sign off depends on how you feel about the person to whom you are writing. Examples include **Love, Yours truly** and **Best wishes**.

Your full address → 6 Cherry Lane
West Park
Maple Town
AB1 2CD

Date → 21 June 2016

Dear Sam,

How are you? I hope you are feeling better after being ill. I've never had chickenpox but I bet it was horrible! My mum has a scar on her chin where she scratched one of her spots so I hope you are careful!

I'm sorry that I haven't written for so long but I've been very busy practising for my piano exam. I'm worried that I'm not going to pass because level 3 is very difficult. The exam is on the 3rd July. I'll let you know how it goes. How are your trumpet lessons going? Are you still enjoying them?

I went to the beach last week because the weather was so nice. My two best friends came too, and we had a brilliant time – playing football and cricket on the sand and splashing around in the sea! The water was a bit cold to start with but we soon warmed up. What have you been doing to make the most of the good weather?

My mum told me yesterday that we are going to visit you in the summer holidays. I can't wait as we always have so much fun playing in the park by your house.

Anyway, I've got to go now and practise on the piano again! I'm looking forward to seeing you soon. Keep in touch!

Love,

Sarah

To finish, sign your name or nickname.

Concluding paragraph: Sign off and invite the recipient to respond. Do not end the letter suddenly.

Informal does not mean incorrect! Always use correct spellings and punctuation.

Persuasive Writing

The following mnemonic shows many of the techniques used in persuasive texts.

		Effect	Example
D	**Direct address**	Establishes a direct connection with the reader	Your country needs you.
A	**Alliteration**	Emphasises the key points and grabs the reader's attention	Smooth and silky
F	**Facts and figures**	Makes the text factual and more believable	Kills 99.9% of bacteria
O	**Opinion**	Helps persuade the reader	Probably the best book in the world!
R	**Repetition and Rhetorical questions**	Encourages deeper thinking	Are you getting enough?
E	**Emotive language**	Makes the text more personal	Show someone they're loved this Christmas.
S	**Statistics**	Makes any claim seem more genuine and believable	Reduces plaque by up to 98%
T	**Triplets or lists of three**	Grabs the reader's attention and highlights the main points	Bigger. Bolder. Better!

daydrea EDUCAT

Persuasive writing is used in adverts and leaflets to convince the audience to buy or support a product or service. The language needs to be clear, concise and to the point to grab the audience's attention.

Use direct address to connect directly with the reader.

Use headings to highlight key information and create clearly defined sections.

Use alliteration to grab the reader's attention.

Use adjectives and exaggeration to highlight the quality of the product or service.

Ask rhetorical questions to make the reader think about the experience.

Use relevant facts and figures to persuade your reader.

Anticipate any concerns and address them with counter-arguments.

Back up your argument with customers' opinions and expert reviews.

Use emotive language to engage and challenge the reader.

Include contact details and a call to action.

Dangerously Delicious
Fusion Restaurant

An Experience You Will Never Forget

Distinctly different and delicious, our menu is the most surprising and delightful.

Choose from over 100 Ingredients

We use the finest ingredients from around the world to create a flavour fusion that will tingle your taste buds. With over 100 different flavour combinations, we have something for everyone!

Have you ever tried bacon-flavoured ice cream or tomatoes with maple syrup? Well, here is your chance!

Award-Winning Chefs

If you are stuck for ideas, our expert chefs are ready to help with sumptuous suggestions and tasty tips. If you don't enjoy the taste you have created, you can try something else for no extra charge.

Don't just take our word for it!

" Daring and different, this restaurant invites brave taste buds to fight and win.
Shaun Miles, *Fenderton Express* "

Book now to discover your taste sensation!

www.dangerouslydelicious.rest
0844 600 1664 | Unit 1, St Paul's Arcade, London

Newspapers

A newspaper is a publication that contains news reports, general information and advertising. It often features articles on politics, crime, business, art, entertainment and sport.

A newspaper article reports an event that has happened or is going to happen.

Research Events

Once you have decided on the topic for your article, research what has happened or what is likely to happen.

List Key Information

Write a list of the key points and create a checklist of what information needs to be included in the article.

It is important to write in a format and style that are suitable for the intended audience.

HOW TO WRITE A
NEWSPAPER ARTICLE

No. 68903   MONDAY, 7th NOVEMBER 2016   70p   WWW.THEBROADSHEET.BIZ

A newspaper headline must be accurate and reflect what the story is about. To attract people's attention and encourage them to read on, headlines often include:

Alliteration	Ambiguities	Omissions	Puns
Where several words in a phrase begin with the same sound.	Where there is some doubt about the meaning of the phrase.	Where a word or information is missing.	A play on words that is often amusing.

Opening Paragraph

In the opening paragraph, identify the main points of the article.

Keep the opening brief but ensure the topic of the article is explained.

Closing Paragraph

Do not end your closing paragraph suddenly. Finish with a closing sentence or quote that provides a conclusion.

Once you have finished your article, decide on an appropriate layout for text and pictures.

Check that the article is factually correct and that there are no spelling or grammatical errors.

Explanation and Main Body

Expand on the information provided in the opening paragraph. Explain, in detail, what the article is about.

Provide the most important information first.

Try to include quotes from people involved in the article, such as experts and witnesses, to back up your story.

Remember to use language that suits the audience.

Use simple vocabulary and short sentences and paragraphs for tabloid articles.

Use complex vocabulary and long sentences and paragraphs for broadsheet articles.

Crucial information
↓
Supporting information
↓
Background information

---

daydrea

Balanced Argument

A balanced argument
is unbiased and
considers both
points of view.

GREENFIELD SCHOOL

Title: clearly state
the topic of the
argument.

Should students be allowed to help choose new teachers for their school?

Introduction:
explain the topic of
the argument, and
outline the main
points of view.

In many schools across the UK, students are invited to help select new teachers for their schools. Some people think this gives students valuable experience and responsibility, but others believe that students may hire teachers for the wrong reason and do not understand the complex issues involved with the interviewing process. To gain a better understanding of who is in favour of this idea and who is not, a range of students, teachers and parents were surveyed.

**Explain the
arguments for.**

Most students want to be involved in selecting their teachers and have a mature approach to the process, stating that they expect new teachers to attend class regularly, teach the curriculum and treat students with respect.

**Conjunctive adverbs
can be used to link
your arguments.**

Furthermore, some parents argue that student involvement will help students become more mature, as long as the "right" students are involved. Others, worrying about the potential for abuse, feel that such matters are best left in the hands of experienced adults.

**Explain the
arguments against.**

Similarly, many teachers are wary of having students involved in the selection process because they feel students may not understand the intricacies of interviewing and what makes a good teacher. One story of how a science teacher was rejected because students thought he "looked like Humpty Dumpty" recently made the national headlines.

**Do not include your
personal opinion.**

**Provide evidence to
support the
arguments.**

Clearly opinions are divided. Most people believe that student involvement in selecting new teachers could be advantageous, but only with certain safeguarding in place. However, others worry that there are already too many pressures on teachers. All in all, I sympathise with those who feel that student involvement is not necessary. Although giving students the opportunity to help make such decisions may help their personal development and confidence, the potential negative effects on teachers are too significant to ignore.

**Conclude with a
summary of both
points of view. This
can also include
your own views.**

After you have finished, read what you have written to ensure that all of the correct information has been included. Always check your spelling, punctuation and grammar.

Report Writing

A report provides a factual description of an object, topic or event – specifically, the who, what, where, when and why.

Heading: the heading needs to state what the report is about. Keep it clear and simple.

Introduction: provide a general overview of what you are writing about. Try to answer the who, **what**, where, **when** and why questions.

Paragraphs: use a new paragraph for each key point or event.

Third Person: write in the third person.

Subheadings: these separate each section.

Tense: use present tense. However, use past tense to discuss historical events.

Cohesion: use devices such as conjunctions and adverbials to build cohesion and link ideas.

Events: events do not need to be written in the order in which they happened.

Conclusion: write a concluding sentence.

Remember: check that all information included is correct. Also, always check your spelling and punctuation.

The Black Death

Introduction

In 1345, a terrible plague called **The Black Death** began to spread across **Europe**. From **1345 to 1350**, it killed between 30 and 60% of the population – **around 75 million people.**

Shocking fact.

Causes of the Black Death

The Black Death is thought to have started in Central Asia. It was spread to western countries by germ-carrying fleas in the fur of black rats that infested most merchant ships of the time. These rats would jump off the ships in ports and scurry into nearby cities and towns. Here the rats would offload their fleas in houses and in the water and food supplies. The fleas then infected human beings.

Symptoms

There were many signs and symptoms of infection – headache, sickness, painful aching joints and buboes (large swellings). Buboes gave the disease the name by which it is still known, bubonic plague. Those who caught it usually died within a few days.

The Myths

Unfortunately, 14th-century Europeans knew far less about the plague than we do now. They blamed foreigners, beggars and lepers – people who could not defend themselves – for allegedly causing this tragedy.

During the plague, many people believed that the stars and planets worked for God. Most scientists, doctors, kings, queens and other important people believed that God was very unhappy about the behaviour of men and women, so he sent evil rays to Earth from the planets Saturn, Jupiter and Mars to cause the plague to punish mankind.

Technical language.

The word influenza was used at this time to describe the 'influence' of the stars in causing what we call a 'flu epidemic'.

The Death of the Plague

In 1350, the Black Death began to subside, and there were no major outbreaks in Britain for over 300 years. The Great Plague of London in 1665-1666 is believed to be the last major outbreak.

daydrea
EDUCATI

Recount Writing

A recount provides a detailed explanation of something that happened. It aims to retell an event, experiment or visit so the reader knows:

What happened and why   **When it happened**   **Who was there**   **Where it happened**

Introduction: the introduction needs to cover who, what, where, when and why.

Heading: the heading should tell readers what the recount is about.

Past tense: write in the past tense.

Paragraphs: use a new paragraph when there is a change in speaker, time, situation or place. Explain events in the order in which they happened.

First person: write in the first person.

Fun fact: sharing funny events and interesting facts will help keep readers' attention.

Adverbs: using adverbs to describe verbs will make your recount more interesting.

Adjectives: using adjectives to describe nouns will make your recount more detailed.

Conjunctions: use conjunctions and adverbs of time to link your paragraphs and help the reader understand the order of events and actions.

Final Paragraph: sum up the visit/event/experiment. State how you felt about the visit/event or the outcome.

A Day at the Beach

On the 28th of May, just before the summer holidays, my class went on a school trip to the beach. The Head, Mrs. Grier, told us that we had been working very hard recently and deserved this special treat. It was a beautiful morning, with a cloudless, china-blue sky and the sun shining brightly above town.

We left at 9:30 a.m., excitedly waving and calling to everyone we passed. After an hour, we arrived at the beach and noisily tumbled off the bus.

Mr. Lloyd, our PE teacher, immediately gathered us together. Struggling to calm our enthusiasm, he suggested that we run around for half an hour while the teachers organised our base camp in front of the sand dunes.

Mr. and Mrs. Marshall quickly put up two tents so we could change into our swimsuits. Sean, the class clown, mischievously pulled the pegs out of the boys' tent, sending those inside into a panic. Soon after, once calm had been restored, our towels were spread out across the white sand and umbrellas fluttered in the gentle breeze.

After everyone had changed, teams were organised for a rounders match – the bubbly, boastful girls against the even more proud and confident boys. Mr. Lloyd refereed while Mr. Marshall prepared a barbecued lunch. Wisely, they served lunch before either group could call itself the winner!

Later on, after a necessary rest, Mrs. Marshall treated us to a fascinating history of how the rocks, cliffs and caves on the coastline came to be shaped as they are.

Finally, we walked the coastal path to its highest point near the lighthouse and gazed at the spectacular ocean views before returning for a much-needed swim and an ice cream.

We had all had an excellent day at the beach, and were very sad when we had to leave. With the sun dipping behind us, we reached home by 6 p.m., warm and exhausted, but very, very happy.

Once you have finished, ask someone who was involved in the recount to check if any important information has been missed out.

daydream EDUCATION

Comparing Texts

When comparing two pieces of text, you need to study the writers' views and opinions, and consider the following points:

Include the writers' overall viewpoints

What are the writers' general attitudes towards the subject?

*Mr. Jefferis was not impressed with the nightlife in Zante, **whereas** Lewis thought it was Zante's best attraction.*

Use relevant quotations

Are there any quotations that support your answer?

*Zane was "appalled" by the politician's comments. **Similarly**, Alison "found it difficult to comprehend" what she was hearing.*

Look for clues about the writers' experience

Are there any clues about the writers' experience?

*Ms. Evans uses complex terminology and jargon in her review, which suggests she is an expert on computer coding. **On the other hand**, Mr. Bowden's review seems to be based entirely on opinion.*

Consider the style and tone

Are the texts formal, comical, or creative?

*In Jacob's article he describes himself as "an idiot abroad" and makes several comical references throughout. **In contrast**, Ms. Razzaq uses a formal tone to reflect the more serious issues raised in her article.*

Mention the language and structure

Are the language and structure formal or informal?

*Noah uses slang and informal language in his review. **However**, Gemma uses facts and technical language to convey her opinions.*

Remember to consider both the **differences** and **similarities** between the texts.

Comparison Connectives

whereas
both
however
likewise
on the other hand
similarly

daydrea
EDUCAT

Write a summary of the differences between the strengths and weaknesses of London and Cleethorpes, according to the reviewers.

London Lights
●●●●●

Visiting London was crazily expensive, but was it worth it? Yes, we managed to see the theatre production of 'War Horse' and stay in a sleek, modern hotel, but were these enough to justify the cost?

Staying in the heart of London will be one of my most frequently recounted memories. However, it is the life on the streets that I enjoyed more than the expensive treats. The streets are bustling with lights, sights and warm people.

Covent Garden is the embodiment of this bright London. Take in the smells of innovative restaurants and the sounds of competing performers. Definitely worth a day out, and not all that expensive, depending on your choice of food...

Sunny Cleethorpes?
●●●●●

Sea, sandwiches and sand: what more can you ask for? Well, I could ask for more, actually, a lot more.

While some tourists seem happy with ice-cream, arcades and donkeys, I would like warm weather, modern shows and luxurious hotels with idyllic swimming pools.

Perhaps I am too dismissive. Cleethorpes is famous for the best fish and chips, family friendly holidays and a courageous swim in a chilly sea.

Seeking to overcome my regrets, and stop comparing this holiday destination to an experience in a hotter climate, I dared to try a donkey ride...

---

1 ▸ Read both extracts (often called **sources**) in full.

2 ▸ Find the **keywords** in the question. What are you being asked to compare?

Write a summary of the **differences** between the **strengths and weaknesses** of **London and Cleethorpes**, according to the reviewers.

3 ▸ Find and highlight the **relevant quotations** in both extracts.

4 ▸ What can you work out about both extracts in relation to the question? Annotate the text or create a table to organise your points.

	London Lights	Sunny Cleethorpes	Differences?
Strengths			
Weaknesses			

5 ▸ Write out your answer, using conjunctions to link your sentences and paragraphs to organise your ideas.

Narrative Writing

Creative writing will help bring your writing to life and paint a picture in the audience's mind.

Before writing a story, plan what you are going to write about. One of your first decisions will be "What type of story am I going to write?"

Genres can be combined. For example, a romantic comedy (happy ending) or a romantic tragedy (sad ending).

Key Features

Characters	Setting	Structure	Plot	Theme
The people who feature in the story	When and where the story is set	How the story starts, develops and ends	The storyline, or the purpose of the story	The key ideas explored in the story

Characters

Characters are the people who feature in a story. When planning your characters, you will need to consider their:

Role	Hero, villain, accomplice, rival, etc.
Relationships	Friends, foes, family, etc.
Personality	What are they like: funny, angry, nasty?
Background	Age, where from, past experience, etc.
Motivations	What do they want: love, power, revenge?

When describing characters, don't just focus on appearance. Try to show what characters are like through their actions. Use metaphors, similes and adjectives to make the descriptions more vivid.

A dark and mysterious figure appeared in the doorway. His face was masked by darkness, but his piercing red eyes shone through the shadows like two balls of fire.

daydrea

etting

When?	Where?	Senses	

PAST PRESENT FUTURE

←———————→

WILD WEST HAUNTED HOUSE

SPACE

When describing a setting, consider all of your senses, not just what can be seen. A great description will help create atmosphere.

"The thunder and lightning crashed down, lighting up the dark, eerie room for a split second. Sam's heart began to pound with fear as he realised there was someone standing in the doorway".

Structure and Plot

The **structure** of a story can vary depending on the plot and how events unfold. However, a well-structured story will need a clear beginning, middle and end.

Middle
The plot unfolds. A series of important events build to the main event, often called *the problem*.

Beginning
Introduces characters, sets the scene and launches the plot.

End
The problem is resolved and the story ends.

Theme

Theme is the main idea or message in a story. A story often explores more than one theme.

Love♥   LONELINESS   *ADVENTURE!*   Friendship

ANGER   Heroism   Bravery

Themes are not usually directly stated in a story so you will need to write in a way that makes the reader 'read between the lines' to identify the themes. You can present themes through:

Characters	Events	Narration	Dialogue	Setting

Narrative Writing Tips

The title and beginning of your story should be interesting and grab the reader's attention to make him/her want to read on. The beginning of your story can:

Introduce characters

Describe the setting

Set up the main event

Starting with a description of the setting can set the atmosphere for the story. Alternatively, try something different to surprise the reader. For example, start with direct speech, with a question or in the middle of the action.

How to Structure Events in Your Story

Make sure your story builds to the main event; the problem.

Use devices such as conjunctions and adverbials to build cohesion and link ideas.

Keep the reader interested by using imagery, adjectives and adverbs in your descriptions.

Subplots, twists and cliffhangers will help keep the reader engaged.

How to End Your Story

The ending of your story is very important. A good ending will conclude the story's plot.

Cliffhanger

Circular

Twist

Moral

Story Writing Checklist

☑ Have I used the correct punctuation throughout my story? (Check capital letters, full stops, inverted commas for spoken words, etc.)

☑ Does the beginning of my story set the scene and introduce the plot and the main characters?

☑ Have I used adjectives, adverbs and imagery to describe things?

☑ Are the events in my story in a logical order?

☑ Does the story build to the main event?

☑ Does the ending conclude the plot?

daydrea
EDUCAT

Imagery

Imagery is used to form an image or picture in the reader's mind. It helps writers express emotions, thoughts and feelings in an imaginative way.

"The snow glistened like stars in the clear night sky."

A simple description does not have the same effect:

"The snow glistened."

Simile

A simile tells you that one thing is like another; it compares two different objects using the words as or like to emphasise a description.

Strong as an ox.

His hair was black as coal.

Cunning like a fox.

Metaphor

A metaphor tells you that one thing is something else. It is not meant literally. It is just an imaginative way of creating a vivid picture in the reader's mind.

She stared with eyes of stone.

The cold breeze was a slap in the face.

The teacher had a heart of gold.

Personification

Personification describes a thing or object as if it is a person, or as having human qualities. It is often used to stimulate emotion and engage the reader.

The wind whistled through the sails.

The lightning danced across the sky.

The sun treads a path through the wood.

Word Sounds

Alliteration

Alliteration is where several words in a phrase or a line of poetry begin with the same sound. It is often used in poetry and advertising to emphasise key words or messages.

The **t**all **t**eacher **t**owered over the **t**iny **t**eenager.

Don't **d**ream it. **D**rive it.

Assonance

Assonance is where several words in a sentence or poem have the same vowel sound repeated.

The r**ai**n in Sp**ai**n falls m**ai**nly on the pl**ai**ns.

Tr**y** to l**igh**t the f**i**re.

Onomatopoeia

Onomatopoeia describes a word that sounds like the action.

Crash

Hiss

Splash

Bang

Plosives

Plosive sounds are short and sharp, and usually involve the letters p, t, k, b, d or g.

Plosives can create a surprising, shocking or hesitant effect. The effect will be different depending on the content of the piece of writing.

The **p**anic increase**d** as **p**eople **p**ushe**d** and **p**ulle**d** to fin**d** the exit.

Sibilance

Sibilance is where certain sounds, usually a hissing sound (s, z, sh, x), are repeated or stressed for effect.

It is often used in poetry and to create an atmosphere.

The **s**erpent **s**lithered through the mo**ss**y way**s**.

daydrea EDUCA

Poem Types

Poetry is used to express thoughts, emotions and ideas in an arrangement of words or verses. There are many types of poem, all of which have their own unique characteristics.

Acrostic

In an acrostic poem, each letter of the subject word is used to start a line of text relating to the topic.

Sunny summer afternoons,
Under clear blue skies,
Magical flowers bloom,
Making me smile,
Everyone happy,
Red roses everywhere.

Shape

A shape poem is written in the shape of the subject.

Clear blue skies darken, grey clouds gather, rain falls to the ground. pitter patter pitter patter

The shape helps create a mental picture of what the poem is about.

Rap

Rap is a modern type of poetry that is often performed to music with a varied metre and a simple, repetitive beat.

Similes, metaphors and onomatopoeia are common, and rhymes are built within lines.

Limerick

A limerick is a five-line comic verse that follows the rhyming pattern A, A, B, B, A.

The first, second and last lines rhyme and have the same metre. The third and fourth lines rhyme and have the same metre.

Haiku

A haiku is an observational poetry form, devised in Japan, consisting of 17 unrhymed syllables split into three lines.

All along this road,	5 syllables
Not a single soul – only	7 syllables
Autumn evening comes.	5 syllables

Matsuo Bashō (1644-1694)

Haiku are usually written in the present tense and contain two sections for comparison or contrast.

Cinquain

A traditional cinquain consists of 22 syllables split into five lines.

Cinquain	2 syllables
A form of verse	4 syllables
Five lines, of two and four	6 syllables
Then six and eight and two to close	8 syllables
Cinquain	2 syllables

Daniel Phelps© www.planetpoetry.co.uk

Ballad

A ballad is a rhyming narrative poem that tells a story. It is structured in quick-moving, four-line stanzas (sections) that contain an 8, 6, 8, 6 beat pattern.

Due to their strong rhythm and rhyme, ballads often have a musical quality.

Sonnet

A sonnet has 14 lines structured in two stanzas of 8 and 6 lines or four stanzas of 4, 4, 4 and 2 lines.

Each line in a sonnet contains ten syllables and is written in iambic pentameter: five alternating stressed and unstressed syllables.

Poetic Features

Hard Frost

Extended Metaphor

Frost called to water "Halt!"
And crusted the moist snow with sparkling salt;
Brooks, their own bridges, stop,
And icicles in long stalactites drop,
And tench in water-holes
Lurk under gluey glass like fish in bowls.

Rhyming Coup[le]
Where tw[o]
consecutive lin[es]
of poetry a[re]
paired in rhym[e]

Simile

Verse / Stanza
Traditionally a verse is one line of a poem. However, it is now often used as an alternative to 'stanza' to name a grouping of lines.

In the hard-rutted lane
At every footstep breaks a brittle pane,
And tinkling trees ice-bound,
Changed into weeping willows, sweep the ground;
Dead boughs take root in ponds
And ferns on windows shoot their ghostly fronds.

Assonance

Internal Rhy[me]
An internal rhy[me] is found in t[he] middle of a lin[e]

Alliteration

But vainly the fierce frost
Interns poor fish, ranks trees in an armed host,
Hangs daggers from house-eaves
And on the windows ferny ambush weaves;
In the long war grown warmer
The sun will strike him dead and strip his armour.

Metaphor

Rhy[me]
A rhyme is whe[re] two words sou[nd] the same. I[t is] often used at t[he] end of line[s]

Half Rhy[me]
A half-rhym[e] is where tw[o] words alm[ost] sound the sam[e]

Personification

Andrew Young
(1885 - 1971)

'Hard Frost' taken from 'The Poetical Works of Andrew Young' - Carcanet Press Ltd.

daydrea[m]

Notes

Notes